REPTILES

CHAMELEONS

BY MEGAN GENDELL

WWW.APEXEDITIONS.COM

Copyright © 2024 by Apex Editions, Mendota Heights, MN 55120. All rights reserved. No part of this book may be reproduced or utilized in any form or by any means without written permission from the publisher.

Apex is distributed by North Star Editions:
sales@northstareditions.com | 888-417-0195

Produced for Apex by Red Line Editorial.

Photographs ©: iStockphoto, cover, 24; Shutterstock Images, 1, 4–5, 6–7, 8, 9, 10–11, 12, 13, 14–15, 16–17, 18–19, 20, 21, 22–23, 26, 27, 29

Library of Congress Control Number: 2022920180

ISBN
978-1-63738-543-2 (hardcover)
978-1-63738-597-5 (paperback)
978-1-63738-702-3 (ebook pdf)
978-1-63738-651-4 (hosted ebook)

Printed in the United States of America
Mankato, MN
082023

NOTE TO PARENTS AND EDUCATORS

Apex books are designed to build literacy skills in striving readers. Exciting, high-interest content attracts and holds readers' attention. The text is carefully leveled to allow students to achieve success quickly. Additional features, such as bolded glossary words for difficult terms, help build comprehension.

CHAPTER 1
GRABBING A MEAL 4

CHAPTER 2
CHAMELEON BASICS 10

CHAPTER 3
AMONG THE TREES 16

CHAPTER 4
LIFE IN THE WILD 22

COMPREHENSION QUESTIONS • 28
GLOSSARY • 30
TO LEARN MORE • 31
ABOUT THE AUTHOR • 31
INDEX • 32

CHAPTER 1

GRABBING A MEAL

A chameleon walks on a thin branch. One eye looks for food ahead. The other eye looks behind her.

Each of a chameleon's eyes can move on its own.

The chameleon spots an insect. Both her eyes focus on the bug. Then her tongue shoots out of her mouth. Her tongue hits the insect and sticks to it.

A chameleon's tongue has a sticky tip. ▶

FAST FACT
Chameleons can catch **prey** that are one-third of their weight.

Many chameleons eat praying mantises, crickets, and grasshoppers.

Next, the tongue snaps back. It pulls the insect into the chameleon's mouth. The chameleon chews and swallows her food. Then she keeps walking.

HANG ON!

Chameleons have five toes on each foot. The toes are split into two groups. One group points outward. The other group points in. That helps chameleons hang on to branches.

A chameleon uses its toes to grip and balance.

CHAPTER 2

CHAMELEON BASICS

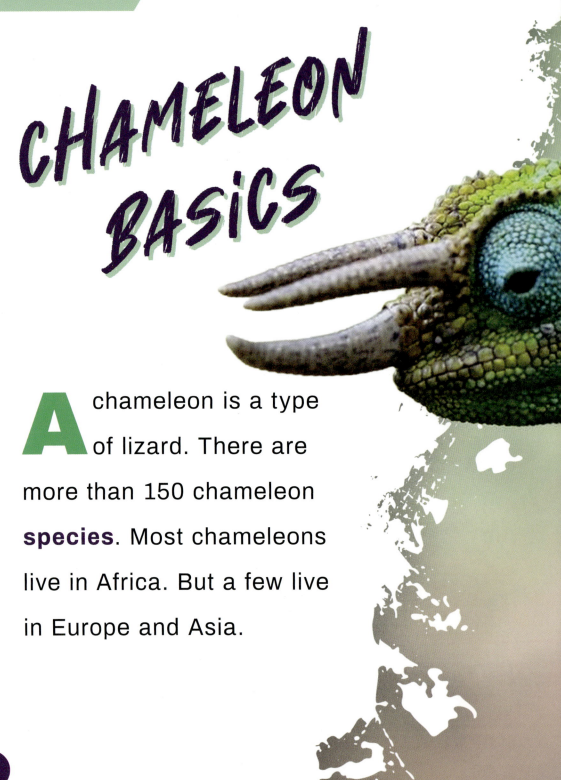

A chameleon is a type of lizard. There are more than 150 chameleon **species**. Most chameleons live in Africa. But a few live in Europe and Asia.

Chameleons can be many different sizes and colors. Some even have horns.

Parson's chameleons are one of the biggest types. They often grow to about 23 inches (60 cm) long.

Many chameleons live in the rain forest. They wrap their tails around tree branches. They grip the branches as they walk, hang, and climb.

FAST FACT

The world's smallest chameleon is the nano-chameleon. It is less than 1 inch (2.5 cm) long.

Smaller types of chameleons live in fallen leaves on the ground.

Chameleons can change their skin color. Chameleons may do this to **communicate**. Their colors also help them **camouflage**.

SHOWING OFF

Male chameleons show off bright colors before they fight. They may turn yellow, red, or white. The brighter chameleon wins. If one doesn't want to fight, his colors fade.

Panther chameleons live in Madagascar. Males are very colorful.

CHAPTER 3

AMONG THE TREES

Most chameleons eat insects. Large chameleons may eat small birds and other lizards. Some chameleons also eat leaves and flowers.

Chameleons usually hunt and move during the day.

A chameleon's tongue is often twice the length of its body.

Chameleons **rely** on sight to find food. When they see prey, they shoot out their tongues. Chameleons usually move slowly. So, they often hide and wait for prey.

FAST FACT
Chameleon tongues are quick. They can gain speed faster than most cars.

Bright green colors help some chameleons blend in with leaves.

Chameleons also have **predators**. Birds and snakes often eat them. It is hard for chameleons to attack or escape. So, they hide. They hold still and blend in.

NO PLACE LIKE HOME

Some chameleon **habitats** are in danger. Humans cut down the forests they live in. Many chameleons can't survive without these trees.

Namaqua chameleons live in the desert. Their colors help them blend in with the sand.

CHAPTER 4

LIFE IN THE WILD

Chameleons usually live alone. But they come together to **mate** once or twice a year.

Mating is often the only time chameleons spend together.

After mating, female chameleons dig nests in the ground. They lay eggs. Then the females cover the eggs with dirt and leave them.

GO AWAY!

Sometimes a female chameleon doesn't want to mate. Then her color becomes darker. This tells the male to leave her alone. If he still bothers her, she hisses until he leaves.

◀ Chameleon eggs have soft shells.

Some chameleon species lay two to four eggs at a time. Others can lay 50 or more.

Baby chameleons hatch from the eggs after several weeks or months. The babies can climb and hunt a few days later. Soon they go off to live on their own.

FAST FACT
Most types of chameleons lay eggs. But some species give birth to live young.

Many chameleons are fully grown less than a year after hatching.

COMPREHENSION QUESTIONS

Write your answers on a separate piece of paper.

1. Write a few sentences describing the life cycle of a chameleon.

2. Would you like to be able to change color like a chameleon? Why or why not?

3. How many chameleon species are there?
   - A. less than 50
   - B. more than 150
   - C. more than 500

4. How would holding still help chameleons stay safe from predators?
   - A. Many predators watch for movement.
   - B. Many predators hunt by smell.
   - C. Chameleons often scare predators away.

5. What does **focus** mean in this book?

The chameleon spots an insect. Both her eyes focus on the bug.

    A. tap loudly
    B. start attacking
    C. watch carefully

6. What does **survive** mean in this book?

Humans cut down the forests they live in. Many chameleons can't survive without these trees.

    A. become a lizard
    B. stay alive
    C. swim in water

Answer key on page 32.

GLOSSARY

camouflage
Colors or markings that help animals blend in with the area around them.

communicate
To send and receive messages.

habitats
The places where animals normally live.

mate
To form a pair and come together to have babies.

predators
Animals that hunt and eat other animals.

prey
Animals that are hunted and eaten by other animals.

rely
To use or need something.

species
Groups of animals or plants that are similar and can breed with one another.

BOOKS

Amstutz, Lisa J. *A Day in the Life of a Chameleon: A 4D Book*. North Mankato, MN: Capstone Press, 2019.

Jaycox, Jaclyn. *Unusual Life Cycles of Reptiles*. North Mankato, MN: Capstone Press, 2022.

Romero, Libby. *Animals That Change Color*. Washington, DC: National Geographic Kids, 2020.

ONLINE RESOURCES

Visit **www.apexeditions.com** to find links and resources related to this title.

ABOUT THE AUTHOR

Megan Gendell is a writer and editor. She likes to take long walks and watch birds fly above mountaintops.

INDEX

C
camouflage, 14
colors, 14, 25
communication, 14, 25

E
eggs, 25–27
eyes, 4, 6

H
habitats, 21
hatching, 26

I
insects, 6, 8, 16

M
mating, 22, 25

N
nano-chameleon, 13

P
predators, 20
prey, 7, 18

R
rain forest, 12

S
species, 10, 27

T
toes, 9
tongue, 6, 8, 18–19

ANSWER KEY:
1. Answers will vary; 2. Answers will vary; 3. B; 4. A; 5. C; 6. B